Essential Skills for
Brilliant Family Dog

Book 3

Calm walks with your Growly Dog

Strategies and techniques for your fearful,
aggressive, or reactive dog

Beverley Courtney

Books by the author

Essential Skills for a Brilliant Family Dog

Book 1 Calm Down! *Step-by-Step to a Calm, Relaxed, and Brilliant Family Dog*
Book 2 Leave it! *How to teach Amazing Impulse Control to your Brilliant Family Dog*
Book 3 Let's Go! *Enjoy Companionable Walks with your Brilliant Family Dog*
Book 4 Here Boy! *Step-by-step to a Stunning Recall from your Brilliant Family Dog*

Essential Skills for your *Growly* but Brilliant Family Dog

Book 1 **Why is my Dog so Growly?** *Teach your fearful, aggressive, or reactive dog confidence through understanding*
Book 2 **Change for your Growly Dog!** *Action steps to build confidence in your fearful, aggressive, or reactive dog*
Book 3 **Calm walks with your Growly Dog** *Strategies and techniques for your fearful, aggressive, or reactive dog*

Your free book is waiting for you!

Impulse Control is particularly valuable for the reactive and anxious dog. Get a head start with your training by developing astonishing self-control in your dog! Change your dog from quick on the trigger, to thoughtful and reflective.

Go now and get your step-by-step book absolutely free at
Brilliant Family Dog
www.brilliantfamilydog.com/freebook-growly

Disclaimer

I have made every effort to make my teachings crystal clear, but we're dealing with live animals here (that's you, and your dog) and I can't see whether you're doing it exactly right. I am unable to guarantee success, as it depends entirely on the person utilising the training programs, strategies, tools, and resources.

What I do know is that this system works!

Nothing in these books should upset or worry your dog in any way, but if your dog has bitten or you fear he may bite, you should take action straight away:

1. Use a muzzle
2. Consult a specialist force-free trainer

"I am not a vet"

You'll see this statement dotted about the book. I am not a vet, but there are some things with a medical slant that I need to draw your attention to.

I do not wish to wake up one morning and find my front lawn covered with angry vets brandishing syringes and latex gloves. On medical matters, take your vet's advice. You may want to seek out a veterinary behaviourist who specialises in this area.

Any opinions I express are based on my best efforts to study the literature, from personal experience, and from case studies. Not gospel, in other words.

Many of the techniques I show you were not invented by me, but I add my own spin. There will be a little repetition of key points from book to book, to ensure that the new reader has some understanding, and serve as a reminder to the rest of us. Ideally all three books should be read in sequence.

All the photos in this book are of "real" dogs – either my own, or those of students and readers (with their permission). So the reproduction quality is sometimes not the best. I have chosen the images carefully to illustrate the concepts – so we'll have to put up with some fuzziness.

Contents

Introduction 1
  Why can I help you? 2
  Where do I begin? 3

Section 1 Desensitisation and Counterconditioning 5

Chapter 1 What does it mean? 7
  Desensitisation 7
  Counterconditioning 9

Chapter 2 Extra sensitivities 13
  Touch sensitivity 13
  Lesson 7: The Five Second Rule 14
  Sound sensitivity 14

Section 2 Look at That 17

Chapter 3 What is it? 19
  What does it do? 20

Chapter 4 Look at That: how to teach it 23
  Lesson 8: Look at That 23
  Adding a vocal cue 25

Chapter 5 Taking *Look at That* on the road 27
  When to use it 27
  When not to use it 27
  Your vocal cue, and more 28

Listen to That.. 29

The magic of this game!... 29

Section 3   Behavior Adjustment Training aka BAT 31

Chapter 6 What is it?.. 33

"I can't believe it!" 34

Chapter 7 Effective BAT essentials 37

Lead Skills 37

Keeping your hands soft 37

Key Lead Skill No.3 Holding the handle safely and flaking the line. 38

Holding the handle safely 38

Long line skills 39

Flaking the line... 40

Whoa there!... 40

Key Lead Skill No. 4 Slow Stop................................... 40

But what if stopping is not enough?............................ 42

Key Lead Skill No.5 Stroking the line......................... 42

A "Stuffy".. 44

Where will we be doing BAT? 44

Chapter 8 Let's get started! 47

A BAT session 48

Your dog spots Dave.. 50

Find it! 51

Carrying on with Dave 52

Looking back over the session...................................... 53

Troubleshooting... 53

Chapter 9 BAT set-ups and variants 57

More work with Dave 57

Set-ups vs spontaneous BAT... 58

Working through those triggers.................................... 59

Some more tricks of the trade....................................... 60

Parallel Walking 60

Oppositional Walking 61

Softly, softly, catchee monkey 62

Troubleshooting 62

Chapter 10 More BAT variants 67

The barking dog in the garden at no.11 68

Somewhere different 69

Stealth BAT 70

The over-friendly dog 71

Chapter 11 Fear of things other than dogs 75

Fear of people 75

Fear of Traffic 78

Negotiating a busy street 80

Troubleshooting 80

Section 4   Putting it all together 83

Chapter 12 What do I use when? 85

Possible situations: 85

Troubleshooting 88

Conclusion 91

Appreciation 93

Resources 95

About the author 99

Introduction

We've looked at WHY your dog is doing what she does.

We've looked at WHAT you can do to start to make big changes.

Now we're going to see HOW to put those changes into action.

No longer are you the owner of "that nasty dog" who is the curse of the neighbourhood. No longer do you have to walk at the *Hour of the Difficult Dog* in order to avoid every living creature on the planet.

This is where I'm going to give you specific techniques to deal with your dog's reactivity - on the ground. Together we will change your walks to pleasant outings, your time on the road will be less stressful for both of you - you'll know just how to keep your dog calm and happy. And when *he's* calm and happy, *you're* calm and happy!

Along with the skills you've already learnt, you will know exactly what to do in any given situation, because you'll know why it's happening, what you'd like to happen - and how to achieve that.

> "I have had a brilliant walk with him today and he was really good with cars, people and other dogs with limited reactions. He seems to enjoy meeting other people and dogs now." Joan and Shep, Border Collie

Can you believe that in a few short weeks this could be you?

Why can I help you?

I, too, am one of those people with a dog who is wonderful at home - but outside was another story. Lacy's hackles would stand up like spines on a porcupine. She'd lunge and plunge, choking on her collar. She'd look for all the world as if she wanted to tear the other dog - and person - limb from limb. For all the dogs I've lived with, I'd never had this problem before.

What made this all so much worse was that I am a professional dog trainer! Someone who helps people get the best from their dog! Clearly I had a huge gap in my learning, and it was urgent that I plugged that gap as soon as possible. I needed to help my dog, and it was clear that there are plenty of other people out there wrestling with this largely misunderstood problem.

So I embarked on further studies. I devoured everything I could find which promoted a force-free approach to the problem. I already knew that the best way to interact with any animal (or person, for that matter) is by encouraging and rewarding the response you want, rather than demanding, commanding, and manipulating. I learnt why my dog was doing what she does, so I could reject anything that made life worse for her, or which debased my own humanity.

I could say my studies culminated with becoming a Certified Behavior Adjustment Training Instructor (CBATI), but that simply marked a stage in my learning. Every dog I work with has an individual history, an individual personality, and an individual owner. There's no one-size-fits-all. My learning deepens with each new dog.

Listening to these dogs' owners and studying the dogs themselves leads me to a bespoke training program for each one. And once you've read through these books you'll be able to choose what will work for you, and your dog - in your life.

Take care, though, if you are selecting strategies, not to throw the baby out with the bathwater! Try everything I offer you before making any decisions about what will or will not work in your case.

Where do I begin?

These three books stand alone, but are best consumed together, in order.

- The first tells you what's going on and why - and some of this may surprise you. It's essential to understand a problem before attempting to fix it. This book should bring you lots of "Aha!" moments.

- The second book goes into the detail of what you're going to change and how, what approaches will work best, and what you need to make it all work. Lots of Lessons in this section. And much of this will involve change for *you*: exciting!

- And the third book gets you out there with your dog, enjoying a new way of walking and interacting with her, and making the episodes you used to experience - mercifully! - a thing of the past. Lots of Lessons here, and Troubleshooting sections to cover all the "what ifs" you'll come up with.

My suggestion is to read through each book first, then while your brain is filtering and processing this information, you can go back to the start and work through the Action Steps and Lessons with your dog.

For ease of reading, your dog is going to be a he or a she as the whim takes me. He and she will learn the exact same way and have similar responses. There will be just a few occasions when we're discussing only a male or a female, and that will be clear.

So, if you haven't already done so, I suggest you read Books 1 and 2 before embarking on Book 3. (And there's a special offer for you on Book 1! Who doesn't love a special offer?) This way you'll be up to speed with what I'm talking about, you'll get much more out of the material, and you'll be able to put it into action straight away!

Don't waste another minute before starting to help your dog make the change.

Section 1

Desensitisation and Counterconditioning

Chapter 1
What does it mean?

Desensitisation and Counterconditioning (let's call them DS and CC) form a common and effective method for reducing fear (DS) and replacing it with something better (CC). It can be a long, slow, business. But if your dog is already used to the language of doing something in order to earn a reward, it will be quicker. The Precious Name Game (Lesson 1 in Book 1, and Action Step 21 in Book 2) is an example of this.

Desensitisation

Desensitisation works on the emotional response your dog is having. Typically the dog is exposed to the thing she's afraid of at a distance or level (if a sound) at which she can remain calm. The ability to take treats is a fair indicator of your dog being ok. (Could you eat a piece of cake while a mad axe-man was running towards you?) Only gradually is the distance closed, or the level increased, as the dog demonstrates that she's ok with that. It must be done gradually, maybe one yard of the 100 yards' distance closed in one session.

You could spend some time on this before your dog is able to stay calm when the thing that worries her is closer or louder. DS will bring you to a level of acceptance, but no further. Desensitisation is at the heart of Puppy Socialisation, Habituation, and Familiarisation.

Imagine you're afraid of spiders. (If you really are, perhaps you'd prefer to substitute mice or something else that won't upset you in these examples.) You are terrified of them, panic on sight of them, hyperventilate, look for an escape route, and so on. Would putting you in a room full of spiders help?

I don't think so. This system is called flooding and is largely discredited - certainly for working with dogs. It may appear to reduce the reaction, but this could be because your dog has slipped into a state of "learned helplessness". He is a victim - nothing he does will change the situation, so he shuts down and suffers it. This, by the way, is why people often tell me their dog is "fine!" when he is far from fine.

You may be ok if we're in a large hall and I tell you there is a spider in a glass case at the other end of the hall. If you can cope with that without any of your usual symptoms, we may be able to walk down the hall a few steps while you remain calm. If we continue, at some stage you'll panic and want to leave. Only very gradually would we raise the intensity of the object of your fear. Eventually you would be able to be in a room with a spider on the wall - without panicking. You may not be overjoyed about the presence of the spider, but repeated exposure has shown you that you don't have to actively be afraid.

The origin of the fear, by the way, is not important. You may be afraid of spiders because one fell on your face, or because your mother shooed them away with a broom whenever she saw them. The only fears we're born with are the fear of loud noises, and fear of falling. Everything else is a learned fear. And your dog could have learned to fear something by association with a totally different experience - a firework went off as he first looked at a child on a bike, for instance. Any child on a bike is now "dangerous". The joy of DS/CC is that it can be used for fears, anxiety, phobias (irrational fears), as well as aggression - whether motivated by the chase instinct or wishing to scare the thing away. It works on the emotions.

Coco poodle learns to watch animals on tv – calmly

Counterconditioning

This is where Counterconditioning comes in. Once the fear reaction is diminished, we can start replacing that sinking feeling with something better. The easiest way with dogs is to use treats to change their response. So the association with the thing they feared changes from "scary thing = panic" to "scary thing = food". If your dog turns to you for a treat when he sees something hitherto frightening, then he can't be staring at it and barking.

Back to spiders: every time you point out a spider to me, or even mention a spider, I give you a reward (money, a token, a star on a chart, slice of chocolate cake - whatever works for you). Gradually your fear of spiders has changed through tolerance, to actually associating spiders with good outcomes. The fear response has died out and been replaced with a warmer feeling about the beasties.

A simple illustration for a dog who reacts to cyclists could be:

- Start a great distance away from a cyclist who is not coming towards you.
- Gradually close that gap (gradually may mean weeks) till you can see and hear the cyclist clearly.
- Start a great distance away from multiple cyclists - perhaps on a hill looking down on a cycling event.
- Gradually get nearer to the cyclists.
- If a cyclist comes towards you, turn and get away.
- If your dog shows her fear response, turn and get away - you got just too close.
- Eventually you'll reach a stage where your dog can see and hear cyclists (not coming nearer) without reacting.

That's all Desensitisation.

This is where the Counter-conditioning kicks in.

- You start to reward your dog for being near the cyclists.
- Gradually let a cyclist head towards you for a while, till you've given your treats, then you move off (two rewards here - one is food, the other distance).
- At some stage your dog will start to point out cyclists to you in order to get a treat. (Don't ask a cyclist to feed your dog - this is too confrontational.)

If a fully-armed soldier jumped out of a doorway in front of you on the street, you'd probably have a shock - and a pretty big fear reaction! Unless ... you live on an army base, or in a war zone. You'd be so used to soldiers everywhere that you wouldn't bat an eyelid.

This is a system that will usually work over time. But there are much quicker and more effective ways - ways that involve the dog in making the decisions, giving her control over her own actions and responses. I'll be showing you these in the next two sections.

In the next chapter we'll take a look at other things you can affect with DS/CC.

In this chapter we've seen that:

- Slow and steady wins the race
- We can change our dog's perception of scary things
- We are working on the dog's emotions

Chapter 2
Extra sensitivities

Touch sensitivity

This little girl is about to stop petting

Some dogs, especially but not confined to, rescue dogs, are very touch sensitive. They startle when touched, they may growl or more. This could be a learned response in order to keep them safe on the street; it could be as a result of ill-treatment; it could be a symptom of illness (get that vet check!). Some people complain that their dog asks for petting, then after a while turns on the petter and growls or snaps.

A good method for relieving pressure with a dog who is sensitive to touch is to use this method, popularised by Grisha Stewart.

Lesson 7: The Five Second Rule

1. Your dog approaches and solicits affection
2. Touch or stroke her gently for five seconds
3. Disconnect, remove your hands, stare into space
4. Your dog will either poke your hands for more petting, saying, "Don't stop - I was enjoying that!" or move away, perhaps with a shake-off (to settle the hairs back down) muttering, "Thank goodness they stopped. I've had enough." You'll be familiar with this response if you've ever looked after small children, who will push you away when they've had enough comforting.
5. If he wants more attention when you stop, you can do another five seconds.
6. If your dog is super-touch-sensitive, make it three seconds. Known visitors and known children, three seconds. Unknown people, zero seconds.

This is a system you should use with your young puppy - and it's especially important that your children learn to respect their puppy's feelings. No nightmare photos on the internet please, of a child smothering a very anxious-looking dog.

Along with the Five Second Rule, make sure your touch-sensitive dog is ok with the Collar Hold (see Book 1, and again in Book 2). Be sure the collar is as loose as it safely can be, and be sure you're not pulling on the collar, only sliding your hand in.

Sound sensitivity

Many reactive or fearful dogs are also sound sensitive. Fireworks; sudden bangs and crashes from building works; high-pitched sounds from electric motors that we can't hear (think fridge, vacuum cleaner). Border Collies, with their superb hearing, are amongst those most often affected - but any dog can react to pain in the ears. You can get your dog used to these sounds by playing sound recordings to them from an early age (conscientious breeders will be doing this with their puppies from 2-3 weeks old). See the Resources section for what to use.

The trick is to start playing the sounds so quietly that you can barely hear them, while a pleasant activity is going on - keeping you company around the house; lying close to you; chewing a bone - for instance. Gradually increase the volume till the bangs and screeches are pretty sharp but not eliciting a response. Any time you get the slightest whiff of a fear response, go back a few steps.

Dogs have been proven to find Mozart (and any classical music from the 18th and early 19th centuries) relaxing - it's to do with the rhythm and tempo. And there are music video channels on the internet devoted to relaxing sounds for dogs. I have not experienced tv for dogs, but I understand its calming programmes work on similar principles.

Fear of loud noises, as we have seen, is a fear we are born with. Many dogs will startle at a loud noise (normal), but some will descend into a pitiful state of anxiety and distress, from pacing - down to quivering and drooling. This could be because their experience tells them that one bang will be followed by many more bangs and whistles (think Fireworks displays). Or it could be that they are more sound sensitive than usual. This is commonly found in reactive dogs.

My sound-sensitive Border Collie Tip would disappear at the first "Wheeeee!" of a rocket going up. She knew that bangs would follow so she'd burrow under a table or chair to hide from the noise. So her reaction was to a fairly subdued but distinct noise which she knew was a precursor of big noises.

You can help your dog in the event of fireworks bangs and crashes, by making a den and covering it with a cloth. Draw your curtains, shut the doors, turn up the tv or specific dog-relaxing recording, and relax yourself. There's no harm in gently soothing your frightened dog, but you won't be able to "comfort" her out of it. There are also calming devices (see Resources section) and calming touches you can use. For difficult cases, consider some over-the-counter remedies for fireworks (see Book 2). For extreme cases where the dog is damaging property and herself in her efforts to escape the barrage, you may need something more powerful from the vet.

We get few thunderstorms in the UK, but in some parts of the world they are so frequent that a DS/CC program would be essential from the start - with the breeder in the litter.

ACTION STEP 31

Practice Desensitisation and Counterconditioning, starting with anything that you can control which your dog finds just slightly worrying. Don't wait for a thunderstorm, where you have no control, and which may be your dog's vision of hell. If he gives forth a cascade of fear and alarm barking at a knock on the front door, you could start by desensitising knocks on tables and internal doors, for example.

In this chapter we've seen that:

- Puppies need a structured program of DS/CC to touch and sound
- We get used to things in the same way as your dog does
- "Familiarity breeds contempt"

Section 2

Look at That

Chapter 3
What is it?

Amber needs to study what she's seeing

Look at That has quite rightly entered the dog training canon as a must-have skill. It originated with Leslie McDevitt in her excellent *Control Unleashed* series of books and videos (see Resources section).

Leslie is passionate about honouring the dog. In the same way that you accept your child as an individual "warts and all", you accept your dog - just as he is. He has an opinion on life, and it's up to the sensitive owner to find that out and respect his thoughts and ideas.

I have four very different personalities in my dogs. There is room in life to give them what they need. Right at this moment while I work, for instance, one is outside dozing on the grass and keeping half an eye on the chickens, one is curled up in a small bed near me, another is stretched out on a large bed just behind me, and the fourth is upstairs in my bed under the duvet. It's not for me to dictate where and how they feel comfortable.

This approach is a huge step forward in dog training. It came at a time when reward-based training was becoming generally accepted - but many people had grasped the method without the reasoning, and were replacing their old "command" mentality (you'll do it because I say so) with a "bribing" method (you'll get this treat if you do it). While that was a great improvement on the punishment-based training commonly used up to the end of the Twentieth Century (and sadly still alive and kicking), it still wasn't a true communication with the dog, and his particular wants and needs.

What does it do?

Leslie uses choice in her interactions with dogs. Dogs are allowed to make a choice about their care and comfort. And this doesn't always fit in with our expectations! *Look at That* is a method of offering the dog a choice over the response he's going to give to something that up to now he has found challenging and worrying. It has elements of counter-conditioning, but is a whole different conversation.

Let's look at your supposed fear of spiders again. If I say to you, "There's a big black spider over there, but here - have this piece of cake!" you, who are terrified of the beasties, are not going to want my cake. You'll stiffen, stand up, crane your neck, look directly at the spider - *you have to see where it is!* You have to assess the level of threat and work out your escape route. You'll push me and my cake aside so you can see clearly. You fear that if you take your eyes off the creature, it'll grow bigger and bigger while you're not looking, then run up your back! You need to look at it.

So with your dog. If she sees something that frightens her, *she has to look at it!* It's no good trying to distract her, holding a treat to her nose as she bobs her head away so she can still look. She needs to assess the immediate level of threat. If she stays staring at it, though, she can become fixated. Staring at another dog or person is - as we've seen in Book 1 - very rude and challenging. It also intensifies the dog's emotions. So we need to interrupt this stare - without preventing the dog from her essential study of the fear object.

We mark the dog for looking at the scary thing, then reward her so that she has to turn her head to get the treat. Now she's free to look again. Repeat, repeat, repeat, until your dog has finished gathering the information she needs, she dismisses the thing from her mind, and wants to engage with you and the world again. I'll take you through a training program in the next chapter, and there's a video in the Resources section that will show you *Look at That* in action: you'll see just how powerful it is.

We are changing the dog's head from reactive to passive. She's able to look at the fear object without reacting. She's thinking. She'll gradually learn that when she looks at anything in the context of this game, she will never have to interact with it. It puts her into a bubble where she is safe. She doesn't have to make those difficult decisions about whether she should use fight or flight. She doesn't have to work out a response with all its ramifications and consequences. This becomes a game she can rely on to produce treats *and* keep her safe.

Because she has to turn her head to get the treat she's earned, you break the stare. This will make life easier for whoever was being stared at, and will help to reduce your dog's anxiety. Her staring will become less and less intense, till she's able to just chuck a glance at the thing that you are "LATting": she has accepted its existence and is no longer afraid of it.

As you'll see, you can use *Look at That* for anything that your dog reacts to, be it a person, a dog, many dogs, dogs running, joggers, roadworks, children screaming, bikes, cars - you-name-it. You encourage your dog to look calmly at the thing that's worrying her rather than have a knee-jerk reaction to it. Once she's had the opportunity to study it without getting upset, she'll usually be able to move on. And she learns a new skill - to be able to reflect before acting, to reduce her impetuous responses, to become thoughtful and make good assessments of the situation.

Life has just got a whole lot calmer! For both of you.

In this chapter we have learnt:

- The origins of *Look at That*
- What it can do for you
- That we have a new way to converse with our dog!

Chapter 4
Look at That: how to teach it

When you are working to alter your dog's response to something she would usually react to, it's critical that your dog learns it as a fun game with you. So you would not start teaching it out in the wild world where things are constantly alarming your dog! The context of the learning will affect your dog's feeling about this game ("Oh-oh, something bad is coming …"). So I like to start this in the house, using something that the dog is happy to see.

Usually this will be your partner or mother or sister or friend - someone your dog likes and is familiar with in your home - but my Rollo the Border Collie learnt it while looking out of the window at his beloved chickens!

You'll be using your marker word "Yes!" or if you prefer you can use a clicker to teach this. When using it for real you'll seldom have a clicker in your hand at the precise moment a strange dog appears up ahead, so it's probably better to stick to the vocal marker. Your dog is already very happy with your Yes and knows that this means a treat is forthcoming, from the games in Book 2, Lessons 3-5. Her head should turn very quickly to your treat.

Lesson 8: Look at That

1. Have your dog on a loose lead beside you, say on your left
2. Have your helper move out of sight - perhaps the other side of a doorway

3. Be ready with a treat in your right hand
4. Your helper steps into view
5. Your dog looks towards the movement that has caught her eye
6. "Yes!" you say instantly, as she looks at your helper, instantly recognising that this is not a threat, just interesting
7. Quickly take the treat to her nose and move her head round towards you - so she's no longer looking at your helper - and give her the treat
8. Repeat

After only a few repeats your dog will respond to your Yes and turn her head for the treat which you always give to her side. In fact, she'll start to become relaxed about your helper and start focussing on the treat. You don't actually want this! So your helper may have to become more animated - jump through the doorway, or knock on the door, or toss a toy in the air - anything to get your dog to glance towards him. Now you can say Yes and give her her treat.

Watchpoints

- You are rewarding your dog for <u>looking at</u> your helper, *so it's essential that you mark the moment she looks,* then give your treat as her reward. We want her to look!
- The key to working with this method is that *you* are as calm as you wish your dog to be. Some trainers have dismissed it as being over-stimulating and getting the dog more excited, not less so. They're doin' it wrong!
- Your words and actions are calm, quick, quiet, and efficient. This should all happen very fast.

You will find that at some stage your dog stops looking at your helper entirely and wants to focus on you and your treats. You will be able to judge whether she's seen enough to form a good opinion of the situation. If so, you can move off.

And it's usually at this first lesson that people desperately want to tell the dog to look - they want to feel in control. Remember we're working with choice training here. So it's the dog who will initiate this game - simply by looking at whatever has caught her eye! This is known as an environmental cue - something in the environment triggers the dog's action. There's no need for you to interfere and say anything other than Yes - the split second she looks at your helper. You only have one word to say - so make sure you say it at the right time!

Adding a vocal cue

It is useful, though, to have a vocal cue for later on. If you remember from Lesson 5 in Book 2, we added the word "Sit" as a label to describe what the dog was doing at that moment. Dogs don't have a verbal language, but they are acute listeners, and very quick at pairing a sound with an action.

So once your dog is playing *Look at That* quickly and well, you have time to slip in your vocal cue "Look at that!" just as she turns her head to look. Follow this with a quick Yes and treat, so you keep the rhythm and flow of the game. You don't have to say your cue every time - just when you have the opportunity you can add it sometimes to describe her action of looking. I'll show you how you can use this cue in the next chapter.

ACTION STEP 32

Teach *Look at That* and practice it whenever you can till it becomes a fluent and happy game for your dog. You can start taking it on the road by saying Yes whenever your dog spots something *of which he is not afraid.* This could be a car turning out of a side road, a person crossing the road, a cow mooing in a field - choose things your dog does not normally react to. Only gradually, and at a great distance, will you start using it for real.

In this chapter you have learnt:

- How to teach *Look at That*
- The finer points to watch out for
- How to add a vocal cue

Chapter 5
Taking *Look at That* on the road

When to use it

Once you have this game under your belt, you can use it at any moment when you or your dog sees something that may worry him. By initiating the LAT game you are putting the feared object into a structure that keeps it at bay and under control. You may just have time to do two Yeses and treats before heading off cheerily in the opposite direction. Your object is always to have a calm dog, not one that erupts all over the place. So if you can get in there with a couple of Yes-treats you are achieving this.

It's a very useful tool to use when something suddenly appears - whether at a distance or close to - a dog appearing from behind a car, for instance. A quick jump into the game while you plan your exit will make this transition smooth and trouble-free.

When not to use it

Sometimes a hazard - perhaps Number 1 on your dog's list of feared things, maybe a black dog (horrors!) or an old man with a stick (Noooo!) - will appear just too close and too suddenly for you to be able to do any more than your Emergency Turn (Key Lead Skill no. 6 from Book 2) and a sharp disappearing act. Remember to make as if you intended to do this anyway - keep it light and fun, even if inside you are churning!

Another time when it's not going to work is when your dog spots something, you say Yes and offer your treat - even holding it at your dog's nose as he stares - and he is unable to disconnect and take his treat. This means one thing: you are too close! Make distance immediately and see if you can try again from further away.

What was it that disabled your dog? It could have been a black dog *and* an old man with a stick, both at once! (See Book 2 on Trigger Stacking.) Or perhaps the dog was returning his stare, and adding in some threatening body language - or the old man was brandishing his stick and shouting. It was all simply too much. Time to make tracks fast.

Your vocal cue, and more

You've successfully added "Look at That" as a vocal cue when you want to initiate the game. When would you use it?

We have a height advantage, so we can often see things our dog can't. (If you're not sure if he can see it, bend over till your eyes are at his head level. Surprising what they can't see!) If the thing you've spotted is one you know may cause a reaction in your dog when it moves into his view, this is a great time to use your cue.

"Look at that," you say.

"Look at what?" wonders your dog as he peers into the distance, scanning for what you're asking him to look at. As soon as he clocks the thing, Yes, treat - you're into the game! A few treats and that black dog that would have caused an outburst from your dog has come and gone - without a murmur.

Now you can get creative. Lacy has a number of different cues for *Look at That* because she can react to a number of different things if they appear without warning or approach us. We have "Where's the dog?", "Where's the cat?",

"Where's the horse?", and "Who's that?" for people, as well as "Look at that" for an all-purpose cue. She already knows the words "dog", "cat", "horse".

So if we are in an area where there a number of things happening - dogs running, cyclists, children playing - and I spot a lone person talking into his phone and gesticulating with his arms as he walks (a sure trigger for Lacy) - I can say, "Who's that?" and Lacy will look for the ne'er-do-well I must have seen. She'll pick him out of the crowd, then a few Yeses and treats will despatch that person as a threat. Lacy is back in her bubble and safe to continue.

Listen to That

And you can use this exact same technique for something your dog can hear but not see! It may be the sound of roadworks outside, a dog barking in the distance, a helicopter overhead, a sudden shout ...

If you want to use a cue, the same "Look at that" will suffice. Remember that dogs don't have the same verbal language as we do, and to your dog, "Look at that" means "Study the thing that may worry you and know that it won't hurt you". You don't need to get into the semantics of verbs!

The magic of this game!

The true magic of this game will unfold with use. Not only can you use the cue to pick out hazards at a distance before your dog sees them, but the time will come when your dog initiates the game herself!

On a walk one day, Lacy started to stare down the hill and urgently back to me, down the hill and back to me. I followed her gaze and saw some riders there, gathering their horses for a gallop up the hill. I called Lacy to me and started the Yes-treat cycle. The horses galloped past us - only ten yards away - and on up the hill. By the time they had gone and we stopped the game,

Lacy was so pleased with herself! She had spotted the horses, and instead of starting to worry about how she should react - whether she should bark at them or chase them - she engaged with me in a game she has come to trust to keep her safe *and* keep her topped up with cheese. Our walk continued in peace.

In this chapter we've looked at:

- When and when not to employ *Look at That*
- How to communicate better with your dog
- The joy of seeing your dog taking over the initiative and choosing to start the game

Section 3

Behavior Adjustment Training aka BAT

Chapter 6
What is it?

BAT was devised by Grisha Stewart. Like Leslie McDevitt and many of us involved with working to help growly dogs, she had a dog who was afraid of many things, including people and children. The existing methods for dealing with reactive dogs were unacceptable to her, as they mostly relied on blame, force, and often punishment - however subtle, it's still punishment (see Book 2) - which serve only to shut the dog down and remove his warning signs. It does not change the underlying emotions.

So she developed a system which empowers the dog to make his own decisions and learn how to cope with his fears. As in all choice training, we support good decisions and set things up so that the dog is unlikely to make a poor decision. And if he still does make a poor choice, we have ways to remove him from the situation quickly and painlessly.

I was trained by Grisha and was among the first few Certified BAT Instructors in the UK. So I've worked with her and seen first-hand the principles that govern her actions.

And like her, I'm passionate about empowering the dog: I don't do things *to* my dog, I do things *with* my dog. Wherever possible - every day, in every way - my dog is given a choice. And BAT encourages good decisions. When these good decisions are made repeatedly from a safe distance and without interference, they gradually become the default response of the dog. Food is used little in BAT - we want the dog to get his rewards from being free to interact with his environment, and encourage natural dog activities like sniffing and exploring.

"I can't believe it!"

People are often amazed at their dog's ability to make good decisions when he is free to do so. I frequently get comments like "I'm really impressed! I thought he would be a nightmare," after their first outdoor BAT session. The system builds the owner's trust in their dog, the dog trusts that the owner won't lead them into trouble: everyone relaxes!

BAT has similarities with Look at That - but in the case of BAT we work in a way that minimises our intervention. In other words, the dog is the decider here - we are only going to intervene if he needs to be fished out of trouble. This goes against a lot of what people think when they first arrive at a course. They feel they should be doing more; they should be manipulating their dog with the lead; they should be controlling their dog. In fact, the opposite is true! And once people "get" this, they find a new way to enjoy being out and about with their dog. They are no longer the minder of an unpredictable and baffling animal, they develop a team approach to the world and its wonders (and hazards). They can sit back and watch their clever dog work it all out.

The joy of BAT is that you can use it for anything the dog finds frightening - dogs, people, horses, children, traffic, quick movements, hang-gliders (we get a lot of aerial invasion where I live, on the side of the Malvern Hills), black shiny rubbish sacks, motorbikes, strange noises … and so on. In Grisha's latest BAT bible (see Resources section), you'll find a piece I wrote about one dog's terror of traffic transforming quickly and painlessly to a comfortable tolerance.

We'll be looking at some of those applications in the upcoming chapters. But first you'll need to know what you need for a successful BAT session, and we'll look at that next.

In this chapter we have learnt:

- The origins of BAT
- That honouring your dog is so much more effective than controlling him
- Whatever your dog's particular *bètes noires,* things will change, for the better

Chapter 7
Effective BAT essentials

Lead Skills

These are of the first importance. Without these you are going to make life a lot harder for yourself. While I'd like you to revisit all the Key Lead Skills in Book 2, I'm going to assume that you have grasped numbers 1 and 2, and reproduce here the ones you specifically need for BAT. And if you jumped straight to Book 3 this chapter is even more important.

Keeping your hands soft

Keeping your hands soft on a floppy lead can be hard to do. You've spent ages holding the lead tight as if your life depended on it, restricting your dog's freedom. This is understandable as you may have been afraid he would hurt someone.

But now we want the dog to have freedom - freedom to choose to stay calm! - and making sure you keep your hands soft and the line loose is going to go a long way towards this. If your dog sails off away from you, you need to be able to stop him without yanking him off his feet. You want him to slow down, turn, and choose to come back to you. The lead needs to stay fluid so nothing sudden happens. Your grasp as you clutch the lead tight and the tension this causes will tell your dog that something bad is happening. Perhaps he'd better bark at the nearest thing to keep it away!

I know you're thinking that if you loosen the lead, he'll pull all the time - but that's the old thinking. You now know that giving your dog the freedom to choose and then rewarding the choice you want will have him making good decisions in no time. As he learns these new skills, things will be changing dramatically before your eyes. Don't worry about your seeming loss of control: you will always have a firm hold of the handle.

Key Lead Skill No.3
Holding the handle safely and flaking the line

Whatever lead or line you are using (and please don't use one less than 6 feet in length!) you need to hold it safely. Safe so that your hand can't slip out, and safe so that your wrist can't get broken if your dog suddenly lurches out at an angle.

Holding the handle safely

1. Hold the lead handle up in one hand - say, your left hand - while the other hand - your right hand - goes through the loop like threading a needle
2. Then, while the handle is round your right wrist, bring the lead up and grip it against your right hand with your right thumb.
3. The line is now emerging from between your thumb and hand. This way you have a secure hold without stress, and your bones are safe!

If this has totally confused you (sorry), you will be pleased to know that there is a video illustrating this and the following lead skills which you'll find in the Resources section.

Safety point: if you insist on letting your children handle your reactive dog, then they should not hold the lead this securely - far safer for them if they simply hold the line and ignore the handle so they don't get dragged across the road. But seriously: don't.

Long line skills

For a lot of the training you'll be learning, you'll need to use a long line. Panic not! It's very easy when you know how. I find that people - once introduced to the joys of the long line - never want to go back to a shorter lead, except, of course, on the street.

This long line is not going to trail on the ground - it's going to stay in your hands, free of mud and wet, and is not going to wind your dog's legs up in knots or be a trip hazard for you or any passing children. You can watch the video in the Resources section, and I'll describe it for you here too.

A long line of about 15 feet is perfect for our purposes - see Book 2 for what to choose. It will provide a connection between you and your dog while allowing her to mooch around in a natural manner, and - importantly - give her the freedom to express her body language. You will always have a safe hold of the handle and a lot of the line, but you can allow your dog to make choices. Don't worry, we'll make sure these are all good choices! Just like the red or blue jumper offered to your toddler, we will limit the range of choices she can make, and weight the best choice heavily in our favour.

So the first thing to learn is how to control that line without breaking your fingers, or causing your dog to be yanked to a halt. This system is known by the nautical term "flaking" - used when the line is laid out on the deck in figures of eight. This ensures that when the net is thrown overboard, the line runs freely and there is no danger of a knot stopping the net from deploying, or of a coil catching a sailor's leg and taking him overboard with it.

You may be in the habit of winding a rope up in loose coils. The danger of this is that if your dog suddenly shoots forward, a coil will close round your fingers. There is a very real danger of breaking a finger this way!

Flaking the line

1. Layer your line, in the hand holding the handle, in long bows or figures of eight.
2. As your dog moves away, you can open your fingers for the line to snake out through the channel your other hand is making, then as you and your dog near each other again,
3. you can flake it into your hand again so it's not touching the ground.

All these lead skills really become very easy with a bit of practice - even for people who have difficulty distinguishing left and right, or who are not very nimble-handed. The long line will become a soft and relaxed connection between you and your dog. It will shrink and grow organically as your dog moves closer to you then further away again. It's like gently holding a child's hand, rather than gripping that hand tight as you might if you were near a busy road with a fractious four-year-old.

Whoa there!

So let's look now at how you can slow your dog to a gentle halt without pulling. You really never have to pull your dog's lead again!

Key Lead Skill No. 4
Slow Stop

1. Your dog is heading away from you, perhaps in pursuit of a good scent, or trying to reach someone.
2. As he moves away from you, loosely cup your left hand under the lead, letting the line run through freely, gradually closing your grip so he can feel this squeezing action as the lead slows down.
3. This will slow him sufficiently to ease him into a stand.

4. Now relax your hands and lead - you may need to take a small step forward to let your hands soften and drop down - and admire your dog standing on a loose lead.

5. You can attract him back to you if you need to with your voice - treat, and carry on.

This should all be calm, mostly noiseless, and easy. It's like holding your friend's hand and gently slowing them down till they come back into step beside you. No need for "Oi!" "Stop!" "C'me here" or anything else other than saying, "Good Boy!" and giving him a welcoming smile when he reorients to you.

Try this first with another person instead of your dog to help you. Ask them to hold the clip of the lead in their hand, turn away from you and let the lead drape over their shoulder, with you behind them holding the line. As they walk away and you start to close your fingers on the lead, they should be fully aware of that sensation and respond to it. They'll be able to tell you very clearly if you're gently slowing them or jolting them to a stop! Your dog too will recognise this feeling on the lead as "Oh hallo, we're stopping now."

When you start, it may take a few attempts to get your dog to stay still and balanced when she stops so that you're able to relax the lead. After a while she'll know that this rubbing sensation on the lead is the precursor to a halt. The right sort of harness will help enormously to get her to balance on her own four feet instead of using you as a fifth leg. See the Resources section at the end of the book.

You may find that your dog slows beautifully to a halt, but as soon as you relax your line she surges forward again! So when you slow stop her, relax your hands just a little (an inch or so) to test whether she's standing balanced on her own feet. If she immediately starts to lean forward again, ease her to a stop again - maybe just using your fingers on the line - and test again. Sooner or later, she's going to realise that slow stop means stand still. The point to remember is that if you've decided she should stop (you may be seeing trouble up ahead) then stop she shall. Don't move yourself once you've committed to stopping.

But what if stopping is not enough?

There are going to be times when you can slow stop your dog, but she is still trying to surge forward. Maybe you're just too close to the thing that's worrying her. So, as you know from Section 2, Chapter 3 of this book:

Whenever your dog is unhappy about a situation, the first thing to do is make distance.

But how can you do that? You know that if you try and haul her back when she's this aroused that it's going to turn into an ugly mess. Not only is it hard to drag her backwards - her feet are firmly planted behind her and you're pulling against her strongest muscles, in her back and haunches (think of a horse drawing a cart) - and worse, just trying to pull her back is highly likely to trigger an outburst.

You are going to love this lead skill! Instead of trying to force her to comply with what you want, remember the red and blue jumpers! Give her a choice!

Key Lead Skill No.5
Stroking the line

1. Hold onto the line and stay put yourself to make sure your dog can't move forward
2. With a hand-over-hand action you *gently stroke* the line as you make attractive cooing and kissy noises. There is NO pulling going on
3. Your dog will feel this gentle touch and turn to look at you, as you bend over behind her in a kind of play-bow inviting her to join you.

4. She'll turn of her own volition and trot happily towards you, the scary thing quite forgotten.

5. Back up a few steps while she engages with you, then you can turn and head away.

It's as easy as that. And people are usually astonished when they learn this skill! Make sure you have the other skills down before you start on this one. Once you have mastered this, along with the other skills you've learned, *you will never have to pull your dog's lead again.* Think of that!

Most of you will have some experience with children, either through having your own, or through having been one. Think of the times you've needed to distract your child - possibly from a dangerous situation - by saying "Is that a *giraffe* over there?" or some such. You get a lightning response! This is the same kind of idea we're using here. Distraction and diversion.

All these lead skills can be done with a short or a long line. I find that it's easier to learn the first two on a short line, and these three here on a long line. Once you've mastered them, you can use them with any lead. For BAT we'll be working on a long line.

It's you who has to do some learning here. Just like driving a car, if you grate the gears and stamp on the pedals your car is not going to perform well. To get a smooth "drive" with your dog, you're going to need to learn these Key Lead Skills carefully. Your dog will say, "Oh, that's what she wants!" and it will all become a breeze. You really will wonder how you managed before!

Whatever lead skill you choose to use at any time, your first response is always: relax, soften hands, drop your shoulders, b-r-e-a-t-h-e.

A "Stuffy"

A what?? I always like to start any BAT training off using a stuffed toy dog. It needs to be a realistic, life-size dog - and there are some great ones available (see Resources section). If you're lucky you can pick one up at a charity shop or car boot sale. Or your teenage daughter may have something lifelike that will do the trick.

Why use a stuffed dog - surely the dog will know it's not real? Actually no, they don't. They are totally convinced. The reason for using a stuffy to start with is that the handler has to learn this new system, and the dog has to learn this new system. I don't need to add something unpredictable into the mix! I know that the stuffy will stay where he's put, and that he'll behave nicely (my stuffies all have identities: there's Melissa, Dave, and Killer, and Puss and Pusspuss the cats). The novice handler can focus entirely on their own dog and - crucially - their line-handling skills. The aim is not to go and meet Dave or Melissa (don't recommend meeting Killer), but just to tolerate their existence in the landscape.

Using a stuffy also helps *you* to relax. You may have spent years walking your dog in a state of heightened awareness, waiting for the ghastly moment when he kicks off. Once you can focus entirely on your dog and not on what anyone else thinks, change suddenly appears possible.

You may feel self-conscious about other people's opinions if they come across you walking around near a toy dog. But hey - they're only going to think you a bit odd (if they notice at all: most people also think the toy dog is real). Isn't that better than their superior disapproval when they see you trying to control a "dangerous" snarling lunatic on the end of your lead?

Where will we be doing BAT?

You'll need a suitable place to start teaching BAT. This needs to be an open space where you can see a good distance. You don't want things jumping out at you all over the place and catching your dog unawares. This does not necessarily exclude towns and streets. If you are using your local park, you'll need to choose a time when it's fairly sparsely populated. You may find you can get access to one of those splendidly landscaped business parks out of hours, or the grounds of an educational establishment. A large and empty shopping centre car park could work well. Think distance. Choose your place carefully, with your own dog's fears in mind.

Also think what your dog's fears are. If she's afraid of traffic, clearly you'll start a long way from any road. If people without dogs are upsetting, choose a place where you're unlikely to see lone people - taking a shortcut home from work through the park, for instance.

In this chapter we have:

- Revisited the vital Key Lead Skills you'll need to be fluent with
- Looked at the approach you need to adopt
- Looked at suitable places to start out

Chapter 8
Let's get started!

Mabel studies Dave at a safe distance

You've got your harness; you've got your long line; you've got your stuffy; you've found a great place to start work with your dog. Now what?

When you're doing a BAT session, I want you to remember two things:

1. Whatever your dog wants to look at is what you are working. So if he needs to study the dogs playing 200 yards away, or the helicopter

overhead, instead of the stuffy at 40 yards, then that's what you "BAT".

2. The object of the session is not proximity to the trigger - whether stuffed or real. The object is to have a calm dog. If you spend twenty minutes wandering around in the area of your trigger and your dog stays calm and doesn't react - that's a successful session! Anyone watching would wonder what on earth you are doing, as nothing appears to be happening. But we know that nothing happening is a good thing. Nothing happening is what we'd like on every walk! So always work at a distance at which your dog can remain calm - maybe alert and slightly challenged, but calm. It doesn't matter whether that's 30 yards or 200 yards. If the trigger needs to be a dot on the horizon before your dog can look and say "Ah well," before carrying on sniffing, this is where you begin.

A BAT session

I'm going to describe a typical first BAT session. As most reactive dogs will react to other dogs, we'll start there. I know there are a good number of dogs who are very happy with other dogs, they're just afraid of people, or men, or traffic, or just big lorries, or horses, or children, or just children playing - and so on. The system will be the same, and I'll help you with specifics later on. For now we're working with a standard-issue dog-reactive dog.

I'll choose a place to park Dave (or Melissa, or even Killer) where he's unlikely to be disturbed, and where I can move around him at a good distance. Ensure that your dog will not have his back up against a barrier of some kind - a wall, fence, hedge, or trees - this will make him anxious as he knows that retreat is impossible. You'll already be fairly well aware of the distance your dog needs to be able to observe another dog calmly. If it's 30 yards, start at 60. If it's 100 yards, start at 150. We are aiming for success!

Keep in mind the direction your stuffy is facing. Face-on is more threatening than tail-on. So start with it side-on to the direction you'll be coming from with your dog.

Now you can go back and fetch your dog. Load your pocket with some good smelly treats - just in case: I'll show you later what to do with these. Fit his harness, attach your long line to the back ring, gather up your line and start heading towards your stuffed-dog area. On the way, allow your dog to sniff and explore, paying the line out and reeling it in as needed to keep it off the ground, but loose. Keep a weather eye out at all times for incomers! If a real dog appears, you are now working that dog.

While there's nothing around, you can pay out some line to allow him to gather information about his new setting. You never want to be at the end of the line, bent double with outstretched arms grasping just the handle! Always have some line in hand so you can keep your arms slack and relaxed and remain upright and balanced yourself. If your dog is a mighty puller on the lead, you may need to stand slightly sideways, one foot planted ahead of you, and lean back slightly. If he is a lunatic puller, then take a turn of the line round your funnel hand (not the hand holding the flaked line) just till he settles a bit. That turn is easy to drop fast if you need to, and stops your hand getting burnt. You may want to wear some thin leather gloves for this lurching dog till he gets more used to the subtle restraint of the long line. Now you see the advantage of acclimatising yourself and your dog to the long line and its wonders way before you start a session.

Head in the general direction of your stuffy, being aware of what else is going on in the vicinity. Never go straight towards the trigger! Your dog can go anywhere he likes - and you will follow him - except straight towards the trigger. So go to the area at an oblique angle, as if you're going to carry on past, being sure to keep above the distance at which you know your dog can cope.

Your dog spots Dave

At some stage your dog will notice Dave (let's just call him Dave) and quite probably stop and stare. As soon as your dog looks at Dave, you slow-stop him and use just the gentlest finger-touching on the lead to ensure that he's standing on his own four feet and not leaning into the line. This is where all your practice with your partner or children pays off! Then *relax the line.*

KEY POINT: *Whenever your dog is looking at the trigger, you relax the line.*

We want him to look at Dave for as long as he needs to gather the information he needs, and we don't want to influence or interrupt that at all! So keep still and be patient.

Ideally, because your dog has spotted Dave from quite a distance, he's able to look, study, air-scent, listen ... then turn away and carry on walking and snuffling. "Good boy!" "Well done!" "You did it!" Plenty of encouragement from you for this big achievement - which he managed all by himself - as you follow him in any direction other than straight towards Dave.

Not so ideally, despite the distance, your dog is alarmed at the sight of Dave. He starts to get taller, stiffer, he's unable to balance on a loose line and leans into his harness, he closes his mouth ... these are all signs that he needs a bit of help to disengage.

If you were to pull him backwards, or shout, that would without any doubt set off a barking and lunging fit. So this is where you use your lead-stroking - which you have also practiced till you can do it in your sleep and your dog loves it. Step out a little so you're in your dog's peripheral vision, stroke the lead, make happy kissy noises, and as he turns to you tell him how delighted you are as you back up, then turn and walk away together. Your next glance at Dave will be from much further away - maybe even double the distance.

You'll notice that in these sessions - as in life - there is no room for "No," "Ah-ah," a raised voice, all of which will have the opposite effect to the one you want. You'd be adding fuel to the fire.

You are now continuing your easy shamble about the area, and relaxing your dog by letting him mooch around at a safe distance from Dave, before getting any nearer. You can always take breaks in your session, especially if your dog is finding it hard (hint: are you too close?). A break could be sitting down in the grass for a nuzzle, or playing Find it! with some of those super treats you brought with you.

Find it!

Usually in a BAT session, we don't use food. Why? Because you want your dog to relax and focus on his environment - not your pocket! If he's used to being trained for rewards, he may start to offer you some tricks or eager sits to get you to part with the treats. We don't want this. But using treats can be very useful as a distraction and to re-set him into snuffly, relaxed mode. This is especially effective if your dog has been stressed, got too close, had another dog run up to him, or had a barking and dancing episode.

1. First make distance from the things that are worrying him.
2. Then take several treats and whiffle your hand through the grass in front of your dog, saying "Find it!" and shedding treats as you go.
3. Your dog will now enjoy hunting down those treats.
4. Make sure you always drop several so he gets into the habit of continuing to hunt.

Working with heart monitors has shown that the dog's heart-rate plummets as soon as he starts sniffing and hunting. This is a natural, rewarding, thing for him to do. And it has the added benefit of being a calming signal to any other dog - which is also calming to him (see Book 1).

Carrying on with Dave

So, always keeping your distance in mind and only closing it slowly and subtly, wander around the area containing Dave again.

Every time your dog glances at the stuffy you will pause him, relax your hands, and slacken the line.

As he looks away to carry on walking, congratulate him warmly. Every time he can look at Dave without reacting makes it more likely that he can look at things and not react in the future. Every time he does react he's keeping this poor response at the ready - so make sure you keep him in the calmest possible state of mind for the whole session!

Remember, we're not looking to reach Dave. We're aiming to teach our dog that he can share a space with and look at something that would usually frighten him, *without needing to react.*

After you've been ambling past Dave for a while, getting ever so slightly nearer as you go (but never closer than ten yards or so), perhaps walking all the way round him so that your dog can take a safer look at him from behind, you can close your first session and call it a day. You could trot off back to the car with your dog - you may want to play Find it! with him on the way to help him unwind. He will be tired - he's worked hard - so ensure plenty of sleep and rest for the rest of the day.

Don't forget to go back and fetch Dave! And hide him in the car again - where your dog can't see him - ready for your next session.

This first session may take twenty minutes or so. Many short sessions will work better than occasional mega-sessions.

Looking back over the session

After your first attempts at BAT, you may be marvelling at how calm your dog is able to stay - now you know how to help him. And helping him means, largely, getting out of his hair and letting him work things out for himself. You are always on hand if he runs into trouble. You may have seen him getting in a little too deep, and if you weren't quick enough to help him out he may have had an outburst. But you now know how to respond to that to help those whirling hormones to settle again.

All in all, while you watched your dog finding new ways to respond to the world, you should have felt your own confidence growing during the session. One handler of a dog who was terrified of people said to me after her first outdoor BAT session: "I felt a great weight slide off my shoulders."

Troubleshooting

Let's have a look at some typical queries that can come up:

I'm getting tangled up in the line

Try some more practice with a helper playing the dog. Then try with your dog playing the dog. If you're all fingers and thumbs, you could attach the clip end of the lead to a chair in the kitchen, then practice moving away and back, turning this way and that, always keeping the line comfortable in your hands.

I get burnt by the line

Try the solutions suggested in this chapter for lunatic pullers. But be sure you have the right sort of line. A good one is inexpensive, so please don't mess around with a length of heavy rope you found in the garage! I favour flat webbing with a soft woven edge, ¾" wide will be fine for small to medium dogs, 1" wide for a big dog. Rope is often too bulky to handle, and if it's fine it's likely to burn. It also absorbs a lot of water and becomes very heavy in the rain. If you find a very soft-woven rope of ½" or so it may work.

You say to keep the line loose - but when we start out he's pulling like a train! It's impossible to keep it loose.

Practice your long line work away from your BAT session. Your dog needs to learn some manners and not pull so hard into the harness. You may find that teaching him Loose Lead Walking will help. See *Let's Go! Enjoy Companionable Walks with your Brilliant Family Dog*, the third in the **Essential Skills for a Brilliant Family Dog** series of books, in the Resources section. For now, in your practice sessions, keep a firm hold on the line and don't advance if he's pulling hard. He'll gradually become softer and lighter on the line.

How do I know when he's looked for long enough and is ready to move?

Your question is good, as you don't want to interrupt your dog before he's done. There are lots of signs you can look out for, and you'll gradually get quicker at spotting them. Your dog may give soft slow blinks towards Dave, he may open his mouth again (especially if of a breed that often has an open mouth, like Border Collies or German Shepherds). He may look away with his head then turn back to study Dave again. He may look at some dogs running in the distance, then check Dave before moving on. He may sniff the ground, turn his body away, relax his shoulders or change his stance. Just before turning away, many dogs will flip their ears back to check the path is clear. This is a good sign for you to be ready to move off with your cheery "Good boy!".

I don't notice other dogs rushing in till it's too late!

It can be hard to take in your surroundings at first when you're focussing so hard on your dog to spot his every signal. This is a skill you will develop, so take a friend with you for now, who can act as lookout. And when you see something coming at you? Just do your lead-stroking or Emergency Turn and happily jog off.

I'm not sure I'm doing it right.

Well, as you're a total beginner it's unlikely that you have it all perfect! Yet. Familiarity will make it flow better. Top tip! Have a friend video your session on a smartphone - you'll be amazed what you'll see that you never noticed at the time.

My dog zipped round behind me and nearly had me over!

Be sure you're always facing your dog. If he moves out to the side or behind you, then decides to take off, you're going to end up with a wrenched shoulder or a muddy backside! So turn and face him at all times, with your hands in front of you, not pulled out to the side.

When I pull him away because he's beginning to look fierce, he leaps up barking. It's a mess.

Don't! Don't pull him away. As I said earlier, this is usually guaranteed to trigger an outburst. This is the place for your lead-stroking (Key Lead Skill no. 5). Once you master this skill you will never have to pull your dog's lead again. That sounds so good I'm going to say it again: you never have to pull your dog's lead again.

What use is this? It's real dogs on the street he reacts to.

We are taking your dog out of the situation he finds scary in order to help him practice his social skills and body language in a controlled environment without stress. And to help you practice yours! Remember those spiders from Book 2: when you're in the grip of an emotion there's not much cool reasoning going on. We'll come to street situations in good time.

ACTION STEP 33:

Get yourself prepared, take a deep breath, and work your first BAT session!

In this chapter we have learnt:

- Two key things to remember about a BAT session
- How to structure and carry out your first BAT session
- That you'll feel very proud of your dog and yourself

Chapter 9
BAT set-ups and variants

Once you've worked through your first session, reflected on it, and watched the video if you took one, you'll have a better idea of where you are and what you're doing. Some of this can sound like gobbledygook when you read it! It's when you *do* it that it all begins to make sense and fall into place.

So be sure to "have a go" before trying to understand more detailed information. You could even try with a non-reactive, easygoing, dog. You'll still learn a lot about body language and how she interacts with her environment, even though not scared.

More work with Dave

You can carry on working with Dave for a few sessions if you like. You can give him a bright bandana or coat, or use a needle and thread to change the set of his ears or tail to ring the changes. And you can get a helper to go up and "talk" to Dave! Your helper can get Dave's tail wagging, have him jump up enthusiastically to greet him, laugh and enjoy his company. You may need to get a bit further away for this - but it'll sure rekindle your dog's interest in this boring, stationary, dog! All the time you are working Dave, your handling will be getting more natural and relaxed, and you'll be learning more about your dog's responses without fear of the other dog. It's well worth getting a stuffed dog to help out at these early sessions.

Remember to relax those shoulders, stay upright, soften your hands, and breathe.

Set-ups vs spontaneous BAT

While BAT should now become an automatic way of life for you and your dog - using it to cope with random objects of fear at a distance, even for one minute at a time - it can be helpful to arrange set-ups so you can work more thoroughly and for a longer time. So you can consign Dave to your teenager's bedroom and find yourself a person and a real dog. We're still looking at our standard-issue dog-reactive dog at this stage. This decoy dog needs to be socially-skilled and bombproof, but not your dog's best friend.

When using a real decoy dog or person, your priority is that all involved in the session must be absolutely happy to continue. This includes your helper and his dog. As soon as he or his dog is getting uncomfortable, then the session stops. It's important that you honour all dogs - not just your own!

Ideally, your helper should be familiar with what you're aiming to achieve, and knows not to stare at your dog, or allow their dog to stare at your dog. If you need to give your helper instructions on the fly, you can use mobile phones if the distance is too great to speak casually. A good helper is immensely valuable - not just to watch out for incoming hazards, but also to give you feedback after the session, such as, "Usually your dog stares then blinks and turns away. But the time he barked he didn't blink. He jammed his mouth shut and stared." You can't spot everything, and another pair of (informed) eyes is always helpful.

If this is an impossible goal, and you have no-one who can help you, then you will become more resourceful in finding times and places where your dog's triggers are likely to be found, in a low density, and with plenty of space for you to manoeuvre. We'll look at some possibilities in the next chapter.

It can be frustrating to set aside a time to work with your dog, you head to the place which is usually littered with people, or children, or dogs, and find … no-one. There's not a sinner out! See this is as a gift: a bit of comfortable, private time with your dog, where you know you're going to have a pleasant outing. You may be so relaxed by this, that when you go home and find you have to pass something usually considered alarming, you will have a positive experience.

Working through those triggers

Many reactive dogs have multiple triggers. So you could be looking out for people, dogs, bikes, joggers, children, traffic, you-name-it. But not all at once!

- One day you could choose a road junction with a low level of traffic, no people, and plenty of space to get away from the road.

- Another day you may walk along a road near a school at school-out time where you can watch children passing from time to time (gentlemen, take care with this one!).

- You could walk outside the fence of your usual dog park - this will give both of you great confidence as you can get slightly closer than usual in the sure knowledge that you are safe.

- You may notice when there is a local bike race or outdoor bike class, and position yourself safely away from it but where your dog can still watch the bikes.

- You could put Dave under a hedge or at the side of a quiet road so you can come across him and work him at a distance. You have the advantage of knowing exactly where he is and just what he'll do (nothing!).

- Joggers are often easy enough to find, but not so easy to avoid, as they will insist on running straight at your dog, expecting you to simply evaporate as they arrive (crash-bang, puff puff, arms flailing).

It's no surprise that some of these inconsiderate road-users get bitten. Get yourself right away from their likely running path, so they are running past at a distance.

- Always remember distance!

Whatever you're working against, whether it's in a set-up or taking advantage of some of the ideas listed above, you will always remember these things:

- Focus on your dog's response
- Measure success by his level of calmness not by proximity to the trigger
- Your distance will naturally diminish over time - don't push it

Some more tricks of the trade

I like to get my students to graduate from wandering around the decoy to something more like real life.

Parallel Walking

Once your dog has studied the decoy dog from a distance and is able to disengage easily and carry on his way, you can move to Parallel Walking.

1. *Keeping the same distance as before*, start to walk alongside your helper at a similar speed. You may be 60 yards apart to start off. There'll be less sniffing allowed here because you want to keep more or less level. You could use an ordinary 6' lead if you liked.

2. Go back and forth over 100 yards or so, turning at the same time, and allow the distance to gradually and naturally close between you. You may take a few sessions to achieve this.

3. When you are near enough, say 10 yards, you could start conversing with your helper. Chat about this and that, but always be aware of

what your dog is doing. If he's still sending a lot of glances towards your helper's dog, it's too soon to get any closer.

4. You may eventually both stop and chat. Keep watching your dog. You could be 5 yards from each other. As long as both dogs are happy, go for it.

5. If all the signs are good and you are confident of your dog's reaction, you could have a very short meeting - if both helper and helper dog want this. Your dog should make the first move forwards. Keep it very brief - just nose-to-nose for a couple of seconds - both of you moving around behind the dogs to make sure the leads don't get tangled.

No.5 is not a necessary step. It may be that your dog will take way longer to want to meet anyone or anything. Honour her choice! Maybe next month … Maybe next year … Only when she's ready.

Oppositional Walking

If Parallel Walking is going well over a few sessions, you could try Oppositional Walking - that is to say, you and your helper are walking towards and passing each other. You'll need to go back to a slightly greater distance to start this, as this is much more difficult for your dog.

Go back to the Dog Body Language section in Book 1 to refresh your mind on this vital information. You'll have a clear view of what your helper dog is feeling. An experienced helper dog is quite likely to switch sides as you approach so he's the far side of his handler. Interesting: perhaps you should encourage your dog to do the same.

Follow the same steps as above, but when you get to No.3 –

3. Start to go in opposite directions, over 30 yards or so. You can make that distance longer if you feel it's too challenging for your dog. Your helper will ensure that his dog doesn't stare at yours - popping tasty

treats into his dog's mouth will usually do the trick to get him to focus on his handler instead of you.

4. Gradually close the distance between your paths.

5. Now this is getting much more like passing another dog on a road! Your dog is learning where to look and how to behave - all on your lovely loose lead held in soft hands.

6. You may want to stop (how far away should you be? You decide) and "ask the way" of your helper. This may involve him waving his arms to point. All good practice for your dog to ignore!

Keep in mind that you are still working in an open space, your dog knows he can escape in any direction. So when you move this to a quiet road, you could be on opposite sides of the road. Choose a more open road, without walls and hedges or buildings right against the pavement - always avoid those "tunnels"! You'll soon be able to pass your helper - perhaps saying Hi or Good morning as you pass. Only move to a more constricted area gradually.

Softly, softly, catchee monkey

"Gradually". I say it a lot. It's important to make haste slowly. Jumping forward may require you to go back several steps. You have the rest of your dog's life to work on this. One day you're going to say, "Wow! Last year we couldn't have done that!" It's a gradual change we're looking for - but your dog may surprise you by progressing faster.

Troubleshooting

My dog is fine until he's actually passed the other dog, then he spins round and tries to nip the dog's tail

You're too close! Way too close. Your dog is doing well to hold it together until he's passed the dog, but then he just wants to make sure that dog knows not to come so close again. Go back to a greater distance: "Can you do it here?" and only close the distance very gradually.

Why do I have to do all this? My dog just wants to play with the other dog!

If your dog is able to approach another dog calmly and have a pleasant greeting then either move on or have an appropriate game, then you don't. But you wouldn't be here if that were so. If you want to befriend someone, you don't start off by shouting and frightening them. It seems that your dog has some anxiety issues with regard to the other dog, and these techniques will help him to be able to approach a dog without doing his song-and-dance routine. Removing approaches from his walks for now can calm him sufficiently to enable good choices later.

My dog's ok with other dogs - he's terrified of traffic

Then you'll do your BAT training with traffic instead of a decoy dog. We'll look at this in the next chapter, but remember the principles are just the same. You are empowering your dog and giving him a choice - then honouring his choice.

My dog was mistreated by people, so he's afraid of them

Again, the same principles apply. In some ways it's easier because you can ask your helper to do just what you want - or not do what you don't want! Next chapter.

We were doing so well, then a dog came running in at us. I panicked and forgot what to do. Have I ruined everything?

No, you haven't ruined everything. Give yourself and your dog a break for a couple of days to let all the hormones settle - enjoy games at home. When you're ready you can start again, at a distance where you know your dog is comfortable. Rehearse your escape techniques in your mind (see Book 2). This is a good reason to practice your Emergency Turn frequently, so you can use it straight away when you need it. There are always going to be loose, rude, dogs. Learning how to cope with them is a big part of your strategy.

My dog is of a very barky breed. I find it hard to react before she barks

Those woofs can slip out very easily from a barky dog's mouth! It would be helpful to teach her *not* to bark, on cue. I start - at home - with rewarding them for barking when I ask for it, then I can reward them for quiet too. For many dogs "QUIET!" means that you're joining in with the noise and they should bark louder! You need to teach "Quiet" and connect it with … quiet. I'm not saying you interfere with your dog's response - just start from a greater distance and get your very quiet "Quiet" in as she's looking - quietly. This gives her a better chance of assessing the trigger and coming to a good conclusion. Having said that, you may find that a single woof escapes when she first spots the trigger then she's able to be calm while she studies it. A solitary wuff is acceptable. A cascade of woofs, not so good.

We start out well, then things get worse and worse

Well observed! The stress is gradually building in your dog and her coping skills are sliding away. Distance! Do some set-ups where your dog is never going to have to get anywhere near the object of her fear. If she does have a reaction, make more distance and play Find it. If she has two reactions, call it a day and start afresh another day. This is a marathon, not a sprint. In any case, don't you go getting anxious too!

In this chapter we have learnt:

- How to take BAT on the road and incorporate it into your daily life
- Gradual progress is the best way forward
- Your dog is going to surprise you - in a good way
- You are beginning to enjoy relaxing walks!

Chapter 10
More BAT variants

You've heard me say "distance" many times. You've heard me say "gradual". Keep those two words in mind whenever you're out with your dog. You should be thinking, whenever you step out of the door, of how you can find opportunities for your dog to excel. Short sessions all help.

Remember that road walks are specifically for training, not for exercise (see Books 1 and 2). "Today we're going to walk round the block without comment," you may be thinking as you set off on your walk - your dog in her comfy harness, a decent length lead, and pockets crammed with goodies. It may appear a simple goal for a walk, but (if you keep your walk short enough!) it's attainable.

The barking dog in the garden at no.11

The guardians of the gate

So it could be that you go for a walk around your neighbourhood and you decide that today is the day you're going to work the Barking Dog in the Garden at No.11. Usually you can only get past no.11 while dragging your screaming dog with you. Your aim is not going to be to breeze past no.11 in a happy cloud (though that will come later - really!) but to give your dog time, at a comfortable distance, to assess the Barking Dog. Keeping mindful of traffic on this road, give your dog plenty of line and let her just stand and watch no.11. When she breaks off and looks to you for guidance on where to go next, allow her to wander a few steps. If she's going towards no.11 slow-stop her and wait, with soft hands. Let her make the decisions about when and where she wants to move, and only intervene if you can see things are going pear-shaped.

During this session you may get within a couple of houses of no.11 without any bad reaction from your dog, the Barking Dog barking all the while. Maybe that's enough for today? Make a note of the tree or fence you reached, and start a bit further back from that tomorrow. Maybe you'll get a good few yards further without incident. And yes, one day you'll be able to walk past no.11 - probably on the other side of the road - with happy smiles and a carefree manner from both of you! I am always pleased and proud when I walk my four past a yapping gateway on our road. My group of four includes two reactors. They cast a glance towards the barkers and carry on trotting by.

If a friend wanted you to come to the edge of a 200-foot cliff to admire the view out to sea, you may be filled with terror at the thought. If he grabs you and drags you even one step nearer the edge you're going to panic, shout, pull back from him. If he lets you go and allows you to get on your hands and knees, perhaps you may crawl a little closer to the edge. Maybe you'll get a glimpse of the beautiful view, and feel able to crawl a yard nearer the next day. This is "gradual". Maybe that's as near as you'll ever get to the cliff-edge (you certainly wouldn't get me standing at the edge!) and that will do.

The view is not beautiful if you are terrified.

Somewhere different

Always look for new areas to practice your new skills. You want your dog to know that they will work anywhere. While you'll need to use your 6 foot lead when you're on the street, you can still handle it softly and gently and move *with* your dog rather than hauling him after you. Turning deliberately in a slow, tight, circle (you stay on the spot) with your dog on the outside can quickly alter a situation - even in a confined space. As soon as you're off-road again you can use your 15 foot line - which you're probably getting to love by now.

Keep your Emergency Turn (Key Lead Skill no. 6 from Book 2) well-polished and fun - it's always an exciting game. And get used to noticing escape routes as you walk, so they're in your mind if you need to move fast.

Stealth BAT

Ned calmly watches a frightening person at a safe distance (note soft line)

As you get fluent at switching straight into BAT the moment you need to, you can engage in Stealth BAT. This is where you see one of your dog's triggers appearing and take the opportunity to work it for a short while before it disappears.

So this could be a dog walking past on the other side of the road; it could be a lorry reversing round a corner, beeping; it could be children running; horses trotting by; a dog sitting waiting for his owner to stop chatting and move on; cyclists pedalling past; a person fighting to get an umbrella up; someone walking along the road talking into their phone and gesticulating weirdly (in your dog's opinion). You can make use of all these things to work a bit of BAT and give your dog some confidence about her environment. There's just one rule to remember here:

Be sure the object of your BAT session is happy about it

That doesn't mean you have to ask their permission first. It just means that if they notice you at all, they should not feel uncomfortable. This goes for people, children, dogs, horses - whatever. A person may even show a friendly interest in what you're doing. By all means engage in a quick conversation with them, but focus on your dog while you speak and be ready to move off as soon as you need to.

The over-friendly dog

Tigger the friendly pup has to learn to greet shy Django more politely

Your dog may be desperate to meet other dogs! He just lacks the social skills to do this politely and calmly. Some dogs seem to get stuck in a puppy-type approach to strange dogs - all leapy, licky, bouncy, paw-y - then give an older dog response when they don't know how to get away - snarl, snap, bark, lunge. They're frustrated by their inability to cope with the whole dog greeting thing. It can be that they fly in with good intentions, then panic when they get there and, not knowing how else to terminate the meeting, they snap to get the other dog away. Or maybe they just start singing and wailing when they see another dog and try to drag you over to them.

In this case, it's clearly when they first spot the dog that they need a bit of help. If you can interrupt the madly excited response and get some thoughtfulness and steadiness in, you can work on the actual greetings later on.

One way to keep this frustration from damaging your shoulder is to allow no greetings on-lead on a walk. This makes it clear to your dog that no amount of leppin' around and shouting will get him to the dog. You can restrict greetings to off-road areas when you still have the lead to help you. If your dog is off-lead when he spots another victim, this is a good place for the Collar Hold (Books 1 and 2), where the feel of the back of your hand against his neck will help to calm your dog, as well as restraining him if necessary.

Remember that we don't ever want to head straight towards the other dog. That applies equally in the case of the over-friendly dog. But when the dog looks, and you slow-stop him, you may wait forever for him to turn away, so fixated is he on the object of his desires. So this a place for Mark and Move. You simply mark - "Yes!" - his good calm behaviour (you may have to be very quick here!) when he first looks at the dog, and call him away as you head off. Yes - it's a little bit like Look at That. You can give a reward as you depart, to help with this. This uber-friendly dog is unlikely to be focussing on you for treats when there's *"A DOG!!!"* in the offing, so it's not going to interfere with his study of the dog, as it might well do for the dog who is afraid of other dogs and is keen to find a displacement activity.

Working this way, you can end up "tacking" towards the strange dog, like a sailing boat. Each time you stop your dog while he stares, you can move off in another direction - never straight at the dog. Eventually you *may* get to allow a greeting. Greetings should be very, very short. Just one sniff, then you mark and call and lead-stroke your dog away. If it went well, you can have another greeting, fractionally longer before you call him out. Always be sure to move around behind your dog so the leads don't get tangled! A sudden tightening of the leads could cause either dog to react. Perhaps after a couple of greetings the two dogs can be a little way apart while you chat to the other owner.

You want to take some of the fizz out of these over-excited stampedes towards another dog, and either the over-the-top greetings, or the panic-driven snap that can follow. Introduce some thoughtfulness into your dog while he learns some better dog manners.

Tigger gets it right!

In this chapter we have learnt that:

- A new life is opening up before you
- You can take every opportunity to build your dog's confidence
- You can now start looking for dogs, instead of avoiding them!

Chapter 11
Fear of things other than dogs

Fear of people

Purdey checks out Penny safely from behind

In some ways this is easier to work with than a fear of other dogs: you can give directions to your decoy person and control the situation better. But it can also be harder! When strange people are in the mix, they get the Dr.Dolittle complex and think that they'll be the one to break through this dog's fears on behalf of humanity. They can be very persistent. A long time ago that would have been me, before I knew better.

So you need to work with set-ups while *you* learn how to control passing people. I have worked with dogs who have been fearful of humans all their lives, and who - after just a couple of sessions - feel able to take them or leave them and not get into a panic. It is a wonderful thing to see!

You work BAT with your helper in just the same way as you start off with your stuffy. The only difference is that a person standing still would be weird - many non-fearful dogs would bark at that. So have your helper mooch around the area you want them in. They can gaze into the middle distance, they can stoop to pick a flower, they can pause and look at their phone. They can look out for incomers for you too. The one thing they can't do is stare at your dog. Naturally they need to be aware of where the dog is, but furtive glances will do. Having a dog-savvy helper, who has empathy for the fearful dog, will help greatly. If they're a long way away, you can communicate by phone rather than yelling.

Remember safety first. If your dog has bitten, chased and nipped, whatever - use a muzzle. Don't take any chances with your kind volunteer!

As your dog is able to wander about sniffing and relaxing and looking at the person occasionally in a calm manner, you can start - over a few sessions - to get your person more active. They can begin acting a bit more uninhibitedly. So they may take their coat on and off, swing it over their shoulder (they need to be observing your dog with soft eyes and quick glances so they do these things when she's watching), carry (apparently) heavy shopping bags, they may call out to an imaginary someone and wave, they may move their hands about while they talk agitatedly into their phone, they may sit or lie on the ground, they may jog or even run past you (at a safe distance from herding dogs!), they may get in and out of their car, they could even play the irrational drunk calling out a greeting to you. And they could drop their hat or scarf as they walk away, then your dog can study that carefully with her nose to get more information about its owner at a safe distance. Don't attempt all these things at once! Slow and steady wins the race ...

If you can only use as decoy someone your dog already knows, they can have a variety of overcoats, hats, walking sticks and the like to disguise themselves and their walk. Remember we can recognise someone at a great distance just by their outline and their walk, so they'll need to limp, or walk slower or faster than normal.

You do *not* want your helper to try to interact with your dog, and definitely never to offer treats: this is very conflicting for a frightened dog. But you may end up with your fearful dog creeping close enough to sniff the back of the person (who's acting oblivious: "I see no dog."). For some dogs this would be a great triumph!

But remember your aim is not for your shy dog to become everyone's friend. That's not going to happen! Hopefully she'll relax more around your regular visitors and perhaps befriend them, but what you're looking for is an ability to tolerate the presence of strangers without feeling the need to do anything about them - neither barking ferociously nor running away in panic. See what one student had to say about her people-fearful dog after just two outdoor sessions learning BAT:

"We're really delighted with the improvements with Daf so far. We have just got back from a walk on the common and on Daf's terms walked round a big group picnicking and she paid them no attention at all. Hurrah!"

Note that she said "on Daf's terms". This shows a very solid understanding of what we are doing with BAT. It was Daf's choice exactly what distance she chose to pass the picnickers. Anyone watching would have noticed nothing - while Daf's owner burst with pride and joy at her achievement!

Allowing the dog to choose whether or not she wishes to interact with a person, and giving her full permission to totally ignore them is going to lead to a confident dog. She'll know that she never has to talk to any strange person, ever. You are seeing now the fruits of Action Steps 9, 17, and 24 - oft-repeated because of their extreme importance. *Show your dog that he never has to meet another person or dog ever again.*

I was surprised to come across Purdey - the terrified dog in the image at the top of this chapter - running off-lead with her jogging owner a few months after we had worked together. Purdey looked happy and relaxed and was clearly enjoying her outing. She was free to keep her distance and act normally while I spoke to her owner. When off-lead and running she had found that she didn't need to interact with anyone or anything - success!

There are many dogs who choose to avoid people in this subtle way. They may not be afraid, but they don't particularly want to talk to anyone. Do you want to talk to everyone you see on the street? They've worked this out on their own. Your people-fearful dog may need a little help to reach this happy state of independence.

Fear of Traffic

Meg ignores the traffic nearby

This is a fairly common fear in dogs who missed out on their early puppy socialisation - we looked at this in detail in Book 1. So any puppy who leaves the litter too late is at risk of this. So also are dogs who are reared on a farm, away from people and roads. This is one reason it's often found in Border Collies, who also have acute hearing and are bred to respond fast to movement. Whether you know the cause of this fear or not, we start from where we are.

Using the same BAT techniques we used for a strange dog, you can start with your dog at a good distance from the road, with just the occasional car, and with plenty of open space behind you so your dog doesn't feel hemmed in and panic. As always, start from a distance at which your dog is comfortable. When a car whooshes past along the road, let him look, on a slack line, then let him carry on in whichever direction he chooses. If he reacts - you're too close to the road!

When choosing your spot, keep in mind things which can exaggerate the experience:

- Rain - makes the cars much noisier
- Vertical surfaces bounce the sound back - tall buildings, walls, for instance
- Potholes or uneven surface - can cause cars to bump, bounce, and rattle noisily
- Bigger vehicles - buses, lorries, trailers
- Build-up of traffic - a continuous flow instead of individual vehicles
- A junction nearby that causes braking or noisy acceleration

So you may find your nice, friendly, carefully chosen area with the odd car pootling by suddenly becomes a speed track full of teeth and fury for your dog. You need to think on your feet! Move away.

Always default to distance first.

I like to start working with a traffic-fearful dog on a large expanse of grass and open land, with a distant road carrying individual cars (rather than a stream of traffic), so the dog can study each one. Gradually we work up to a junction with more of a flow of traffic - two or three vehicles at a time - but still plenty of open space to retire into whenever the dog needs a break. City streets would come much later. And walking along roads in the dark. A lot of dogs are afraid of the dark.

Negotiating a busy street

This can be hard for the reactive dog. All his fears are coming at him at once! You need to be continually aware of what he's seeing and what needs evasive action. You may think your dog is "fine" in the town centre - which surprises you when you consider his reaction to a single person you encounter on a less busy road.

But look at it this way: if an army brandishing sabres was bearing down on you, you'd lie low and hope they wouldn't bother with you - no point in fighting back. One person approaching - you just might be able to scare them off. Your dog may be creeping on eggshells while you think he's "fine". Do more BATwork with him so he can work out a new way to respond to what previously frightened him. Then you can re-introduce him to busier places a little at a time.

Troubleshooting

My dog just lies down. She's not afraid, she's just stubborn.

Oh oh oh. Dogs are not "stubborn". They don't do things to spite you. If she's lying down in the face of … whatever it is that worries her, she's wanting to disappear through that hole in the ground we'd welcome when something upsetting or embarrassing happens to us. This is common in young puppies. She's telling you she is not comfortable about going any further. You need to find out just what it is she's afraid of, then try and isolate that trigger and work on it alone. If going for a walk means strange dogs, barking dogs, traffic, people greeting her, car doors slamming, children running about … it's all too much for her. Give her a holiday from walks along that clifftop, relieve her of her "terror run", and start working through this book series from Book 1.

I can't always be training my dog - life goes on!

Indeed it does, but it doesn't necessarily have to involve your dog - until he's happy to take part. Once your BAT is going fluently, you can use it on walks with a shorter lead too. See a dog (person/jogger/car etc) and slow-stop your dog. Just stand with a loose lead and let him study the other dog. When he relaxes and glances at you to say "I'm ok with this," you can carry on walking. One day you won't even need to pause.

We had builders in, coming and going all the time. My dog's not mad about visitors so we shut him in another room, but he got out and bit a builder's bum. Have I now got to muzzle him at home?

Your dog is not mad about visitors, then he had to experience a veritable invasion! His stress levels were off the chart, and he was imprisoned as well. This is Trigger Stacking (Book 2) writ large. Get him used to meeting visitors again, on lead. Use Key Lead Skill No.2: Parking (Book 2) to ensure hands-off control. If he doesn't want to meet the visitor, let him choose to go in his crate or another room with something to chew to relieve the tension. And meanwhile work on People BAT at a safe distance outside the house. No, no need to muzzle him at home. The lead will keep your visitors safe.

My dog is quite happy to walk about the local shopping area with me in the daytime. But at night when it's nearly empty she'll bark at everything!

You're probably happy and relaxed walking about the shops amongst the bustle of mothers with pushchairs, old men with sticks, delivery men carrying parcels, cyclists, teenagers larking about after school, and so on. The busy-ness and mass of people is normal. But at night, that place is deserted. It's quiet. You see a person emerging from a doorway down the street: what's he doing? why is he there? is he a danger? Dogs are designed to notice things that are out of place. In a crush of people everything melds together. In the empty street, one person is out of place. And needs to be barked at!

My dog will sniff a new person, then jump back barking

Sounds as if it's all moving a bit fast for her. Perhaps the person moved, tried to stroke your dog, bent over, spoke, or - horror of horrors! - looked straight at her. Always allow your fearful dog to make the first move towards a person. And ensure that she has enough lead to move away behind you if she wishes. Teaching her the Carwash game (Book 2, Lesson 6) will enable her to find her safe place herself if she feels the need. If the person will do what you say, you can ask them to drop their hand down by their side for your dog to sniff. But they may do no more! Your dog can sniff their hand if she wishes, and come back to you. When you meet a stranger, you may shake hands with them, or just nod and smile. What would you do if they moved into your space, ruffled your hair, patted your bum (!), stared straight into your eyes? I don't know why dogs are expected to be people's playthings and tolerate stuff we would not tolerate ourselves.

In this chapter we've learnt:

- How to help the people-fearful dog gain confidence round people
- How to help your traffic-fearful dog manage in our busy, noisy, world
- To put ourselves in our dog's paws and see how it feels for us

Section 4

Putting it all together

Chapter 12
What do I use when?

So you've learnt four key methods for changing your reactive dog to a happier companion:

- Desensitisation and Counterconditioning
- Look at That
- Emergency Turn
- BAT

You are armed to the teeth with techniques - but which one should you use where? How to decide in the heat of the moment what you should do?

As a general rule, use the least intrusive method at any time. Keep out of the way and let your dog learn to cope and work things out for himself. But remember too, that discretion is the better part of valour! Be prepared to intervene to rescue your dog when it seems necessary. Don't wait till he's already anxious and barking.

Possible situations:

There are horses coming towards us, and their teenage riders are chatting to each other and not watching out!

Get out of their path and play Look at That till they've passed. Remember the story of Lacy and the horses in Chapter 5 of this book? When Lacy first saw horses she thought they were monsters from the deep that had to be chased away - this not helped by riders cantering straight past us with no warning. Now she sees them as a vicarious source of food, and no longer a worry.

Cyclists! There's a whole load of them heading straight at us.

You may be able to move off the road and post treats into your dog's mouth as they pass. If your dog won't take the treats, you're too close - make distance! Remember that the ability to take treats is a good gauge of your dog's state of mind.

The park is pretty empty except for a group of dog walkers on the far side

This is an excellent time to do a bit of Stealth BAT. You can gradually wander in a random fashion towards the other side of the park, with your dog making calm decisions all the while. You may even get within 20 yards of them before moving off after your very satisfactory session. Take care if the dogs are loose - they may run up to investigate. But if you can see their approach is friendly, and your dog has no history of biting, this could be the perfect time to have a greeting. After all, your dog has just spent at least ten minutes studying these dogs and hasn't felt the need to defend himself. Be sure your line is slack while they meet, keep behind your dog to avoid the line tangling with legs and necks, and stroke the lead and move off swiftly after a very short greeting. Very short? Say 5 seconds. Just your body movement may be enough to prompt your dog to come with you. If it went well, you can always have another greeting - perhaps another day.

I'm walking through the car park and a dog appears round the next car

Look at That would be my weapon of choice here. But if the dog looks as though it's come straight off your dog's personal "Wanted" poster of undesirable dogs, call out "Happy!" and go for the Emergency Turn instead.

As I walk through our residential area, dog walkers can come up behind us

Cross the road, then do some Parallel Walking with the other dog. This is no longer a situation to fear, but a situation to use as a training opportunity! Peel away if the other dog appears anxious.

I'm walking through town when a gaggle of small children cry "Goggie!" and wobble towards us, arms in the air.

Emergency Turn! And if they persist in chasing, ask the parents to call them back. The most stable dog could be alarmed by this! I was waiting for a friend outside a shop one time. After *three* Emergency Turns in the face of a shrieking toddler intent on "goggie-ing" Lacy, I was amazed to hear the father explain to his wife that he had to hang on to the child now because "that dog growled at her". Doting parents can be a danger to their children.

Incoming dog, with cries from the distant owner of "It's ok, my dog is friendly!"

This is the bane of many reactive dog owners' lives. See Books 1 and 2 for extensive escape methods. If it's too late and the dog has reached you, relax and back off while you prepare for your "House is on fire!" recall. I tend to call Lacy in and slip my hand into her collar, holding it very loosely but with the back of my hand reassuringly against her neck. Sometimes I ask both Lacy and Coco (the reactive members of my team) for a sit beside me - preferably off the path - till the other dog has gone by. An answer to "My dog is friendly,"? "Well, my dog is not." It may work, but it doesn't do to antagonise the other owner. Incoming wild dogs is a fact of life, and we have to learn how to cope with it, without panicking and making the situation ten times worse.

Don't get caught out when something happens. On your walks you can rehearse the various options: imagine the wobbly toddler, the galloping horses, the thoughtless jogger, and practice your technique then.

Troubleshooting

The moment she sees a strange dog - even at a distance - she starts barking. What do I do?

You have to slide your response in before the first woof emerges! You need to be very quick, notice the other dog first and be ready with your "Yes!". I'd choose Look at That here, to start with. If your dog is super-barky at the best of times you may allow one woof to escape as you mark and treat. After your dog has got over the initial fright, you may decide to move to BAT, possibly making distance all the while.

She doesn't bark and lunge any more, but she does stay staring at the dog for ages.

Fantastic progress! Very well done! The staring may be serving to intimidate the other dog - but it may also annoy him. When accompanied by calming signals, like blinks, lip-licks, and lookaways, it's also an indicator of how long your dog needs to assess the level of threat this dog presents – it's often very much longer than we allow. You can move away and let her study him from a greater distance. Practice your lead-stroking with your dog frequently as a game, so that her knee-jerk reaction to feeling movement on the line is to turn and face you. This can then become another of your handy interrupters. If you leave your dog staring for too long, she can get fixated and feel she has to do something. You don't want to head back to barking and lunging again!

When we pass a person close up - especially at night - just as they draw level my dog leaps up to grab them - help!

Don't pass a person close up! For now. If your dog has bitten then he should be muzzled when out. If not, try teaching your dog to wear a head halter (use the exact same technique for acclimatising to a muzzle - see Resources). This will give you control of the head, so if you are forced to pass someone within leaping distance you can shorten your lead and distract your dog.

"Happy!" has become such a favourite game that I can even use it to get a fast recall when he's off-lead!

That's great to hear! Repetition of these games - always as fun - is so profitable. Now you haven't just got a way to get out of trouble fast, you've got a new way to connect with your dog.

My dog's getting really quick at Look at That, so we tend to use that all the time

That's good that you find it so useful. But at this stage you need to be practicing all the techniques. They all work slightly differently, and you'll find a good time for each of them. Don't sell yourself short by opting for only one!

In this chapter you've learnt:

- When to apply your new skills
- To put them all together in your toolbox so you can pluck out the one you need in an instant
- Which techniques work best for you at this stage
- That keeping calm yourself is essential
- Distance, distance, distance - always distance!

Conclusion

We've arrived at the end of our journey through these pages. But it's not the end of the road for you and your dog - it's just the beginning!

If you've just read through these books for the first time, you're now ready to go back to the beginning, get the equipment you need, and start on the Lessons and Action Steps. You should find it all *even easier* to follow when you read it again. This is good. This means you are absorbing the information and letting it become part of how you think. The ideas are not novel and weird any more - they make sense.

By now you will be viewing your dog through new eyes. You will feel for him. You'll understand why he's doing what he's doing, and how you can help him make better choices and give both of you a better life.

And you'll understand why Choice Training is the way to go. It's the way we work with our family and friends, and what's your dog if not both family and friend? Using Choice Training will affect every part of your life with your dog. So much stress and strain and so many of those little daily niggles will have been removed. Life is so much more pleasant without totally unnecessary battles, confrontations, and shouting matches!

And when you're out, you're no longer waiting with a fast-beating heart for Something to Happen. You know now how to manage your walks so that Absolutely Nothing Happens!

Always look for a calm response from your dog. Always make distance - and don't worry, the distance will gradually close. After a while you will be hunting out those places you've always avoided, where you'll find dogs to practice! See what this terrier's owners said:

> "He is now able to look at other dogs and move away with us to continue his walk. This is a massive improvement in just a few weeks. It means that we no longer avoid dogs, but in fact go out looking for them so that we can work on his training."

Walking your dog is no longer a trial and a chore. Walking with your friend becomes a pleasure you look forward to. Remember the joy when you first got your dog? Keep in mind how she's a Brilliant Family Dog at home.

> "My dog is a great dog and becoming a great dog outdoors. I feel we've cracked most of what needs doing and her nervousness around other dogs is diminishing."

Before you leave, make sure you check out the Resources section - there's masses there to help you.

Any questions? You'll find me at beverley@brilliantfamilydog.com I'll usually reply within a couple of days. If you haven't heard from me in a week, write again. It means I was buried in email and your first one slipped down a crack.

And don't go without your free book!

Appreciation

I want to offer thanks to all those who have helped me get where I am in my life with dogs:

- First of all, my own long-suffering dogs! They have taught me so much when I've taken the time to listen.
- My reactive dog Lacy who is a star and has opened up a new world for me.
- My students, who have shown me how they learn best, enabling me to give them what they need to know in a way that works for them.
- Some legendary teachers, principal amongst them: Sue Ailsby, Leslie McDevitt, Grisha Stewart, Chirag Patel, Susan Garrett. I wholeheartedly recommend them. They are trailblazers.

Resources

You know now that there's light at the end of this tunnel! And to discover that the tunnel is much shorter than you think, get the next two parts of the puzzle here:

Essential Skills for your *Growly* but Brilliant Family Dog series
Book 1 **Why is my Dog so Growly?** *Teach your fearful, aggressive, or reactive dog confidence through understanding*
Book 2 **Change for your Growly Dog!** *Action steps to build confidence in your fearful, aggressive, or reactive dog*

For a very thorough, in-depth, approach, where I will be on hand to answer all your questions, go to

brilliantfamilydog.teachable.com

where you'll find info about the online course which takes all this to the next level, giving you personal support and encouragement as well as all the lessons and techniques you need to change your life with your Growly Dog.

For a free taster course: **www.brilliantfamilydog.com/growly**

And for loads of articles on Growly Dogs and Choice Training, go to **www.brilliantfamilydog.com** where you'll also find a course on solving everyday dog and puppy problems.

You'll also find the **Essential Skills for a Brilliant Family Dog** series of e-books helpful. Take a holistic view of your relationship with your dog and work on new skills inside the house as well as when you're out. If your dog has always had to be kept on lead because you were afraid he was not safe, you'll definitely need Book 4 for your new life!

Book 1 Calm Down! *Step-by-Step to a Calm, Relaxed, and Brilliant Family Dog*
Book 2 Leave it! *How to teach Amazing Impulse Control to your Brilliant Family Dog*
Book 3 Let's Go! *Enjoy Companionable Walks with your Brilliant Family Dog*
Book 4 Here Boy! *Step-by-step to a Stunning Recall from your Brilliant Family Dog*

And you'll be pleased to know that Book 1 is currently free at all e-book stores!

Here are the links to all the resources mentioned in this book:

Books by other authors:

Control Unleashed: Creating a Focused and Confident Dog by Leslie McDevitt, pub Clean Run Productions LLC, 2007 **http://controlunleashed.net/book.html**

Behavior Adjustment Training 2.0: New Practical Techniques for Fear, Frustration, and Aggression in Dogs by Grisha Stewart, pub Dogwise Publishing, 2016

Websites:
www.muzzleupproject.com - all things muzzle
www.goodfordogs.co.uk/products - Wiggles Wags and Whiskers Freedom Harness - UK and Europe [This is me. If you buy from me I will benefit financially, but it won't cost you any more.]
http://2houndswholesale.com/Where-to-Buy.html - Wiggles Wags and Whiskers Freedom Harness - rest of the world

http://youtu.be/_32dEnE7UIc - Lead-handling Techniques how-to video

https://www.youtube.com/watch?v=Mtn-BeI9lHE - *Pattern Games: Clicking for Confidence and Connection* by Leslie McDevitt, dvd 2011, Tawzer Dog LLC

http://www.melissaanddoug.com/product_list/1018276.1129966.33560.0.0/Dogs_%26amp%3B_Cats - wonderfully realistic stuffed dog and cat decoys

http://youtu.be/K9yOCb3rzOo Lacy works Look at That

1 yard = 0.9 metres

100 yards = 91 metres, much the same for our purposes

100 feet = 30 yards

Don't go without your free book!

Impulse Control is particularly valuable for the reactive and anxious dog. Get a head start with your training by developing astonishing self-control in your dog! Change your dog from quick on the trigger, to thoughtful and reflective.

Go now and get your step-by-step book absolutely free at
Brilliant Family Dog
www.brilliantfamilydog.com/freebook-growly

About the author

I've been training dogs for many years. First for competitive dog sports and over time to be stellar family pets. For most of my life, I've lived with up to four dogs, so I'm well used to getting a multi-dog household to run smoothly. It soon became clear that a force-free approach was by far the most successful, effective, and rewarding for me and the dogs. I've done the necessary studying for my various qualifications - for rehab of anxious and fearful "aggressive" dogs, early puppy development, and learning theory and its practical applications. I am continually studying and learning this endlessly amazing subject!

There are some superb teachers and advocates of force-free dog training, and you'll find those I am particularly indebted to in the Appreciation Section. Some of the methods I show you are well-known in the force-free dog training community, while many have my own particular twist.

A lot of my learning has come through the Puppy Classes, Puppy Walks, and Growly Dog Courses I teach. These dog-owners are not looking for competition-standard training; they just want a Brilliant Family Dog they can take anywhere. It's a particular joy for me to see a Growly Dog who arrived at the first session a reactive bundle of nerves and fear, who ends up able to cope with almost anything the world chucks his way - becoming a relaxed and happy dog with a confident owner in the process.

Working with real dogs and their real owners keeps me humble - and resourceful! It's no good being brilliant at training dogs if you can't convey this enthusiasm and knowledge to the person the dog has to live with. So I'm grateful for everything my students have taught me about how they learn best.

Beverley Courtney BA(Hons) CBATI CAP2 MAPDT(UK) PPG
www.brilliantfamilydog.com

Made in the USA
San Bernardino, CA
14 April 2017